STARTERS
PEOPLE

Hannibal

Macdonald Educational

These children are visiting Carthage.
Carthage is in North Africa.
They have come to see the ruins
of a great port.

2

Long ago Carthage was a great port.
The people of Carthage had many ships.
Their navy was very powerful.

The Romans were enemies
of the people of Carthage.
They fought on land and sea.
Carthage was defeated.
Their navy was destroyed.

4

The army of Carthage was led by Hamilcar.
He hated the Romans.
He took his son, Hannibal, to the temple.
He made him promise to fight the Romans.

5

Many years later, when Hamilcar died,
Hannibal became the leader of the army.
He remembered his promise to his father.
He made plans to fight the Romans.

6

Hannibal and his large army
started out on their journey to Rome.
They took forty elephants with them.

The army marched into France.
They came to a fast flowing river.
It was called the River Rhône.

8

raft

Hannibal took all the boats
he could find for his soldiers.
They made rafts for the elephants.
Some of the elephants were frightened.
They jumped into the water.

The army marched up into the Alps.
The track was narrow.
They were attacked by enemies.

Some men offered to guide Hannibal's army.
The men took the army through a gorge.
It was a trap.
Most of Hannibal's army escaped.

They reached the top of the mountain pass.
The soldiers were very tired.
Hannibal showed them
they did not have much farther to go.
This cheered the men up.

12

The army started down the mountain.
The track was narrow and steep.
It was hidden by snow and ice.

In one place,
a landslide had carried the path away.
The horses and elephants could not
get down.

14

The soldiers had to rebuild the path.
It took them four days.
Many elephants froze.

Celtic chief

Hannibal and his men reached Italy.
The Romans came to fight them.
Hannibal's army won.
Hannibal needed more soldiers.
Many people joined him.

The army marched towards Rome.
They had to cross a river.
The ground was very swampy.
Hannibal was ill.
He became blind in one eye.

A Roman army had followed Hannibal.
Hannibal set up camp on a hillside
near Lake Trasimeno.
His army lay in wait for the Romans.
A heavy mist hid them.

18

When the Romans arrived,
Hannibal's men charged down the hill.
They drove many of the Romans
into the lake.

The Romans sent the biggest army
they could collect to fight Hannibal.
Two generals led the army.
Hannibal beat them in one great battle.

20

Many cities joined sides with Hannibal
when they heard about his victory.
Hannibal rode in triumph into Capua.
Capua was the largest town in Italy.

Capua

siege
tower

giant
catapult

Hannibal left Capua to capture more towns.
While Hannibal was away,
the Romans surrounded Capua.

22

Roman camp

Hannibal's cavalry

ditches

Hannibal could not get back into Capua,
so he marched to Rome.
He hoped the Romans would leave Capua
and come after him.
But they stayed where they were.

23

Hannibal sent for his brother Hasdrubal,
who brought another army from Spain.
Before the army could reach Hannibal
it was defeated by the Romans.

24

The Romans were afraid to fight
Hannibal in Italy.
They attacked Carthage instead.
Hannibal went back to save the city.
His weak army was defeated.

clay

glue

paints

card

Hannibal rode on an elephant.
See if you can make your own elephant.

26

Index

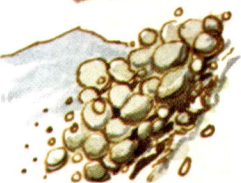

Hannibal's battles against the Romans

Battle of Ticinus
The Roman army was led by the consul, Publius Cornelius SCIPIO. Scipio was wounded. Hannibal won the battle.

Battle of Trebbia
Two Roman consular armies led by Tiberius SEMPRONIUS Longus were defeated by Hannibal.

Battle of Lake Trasimeno
Hannibal won this battle. The Roman consul Gaius FLAMINIUS Nepos and most of his army were killed.

Battle of Cannae
The Romans wanted to beat Hannibal for once and for all. They sent two generals, Caius Terentius VARRO and Lucius AEMILIUS PAULUS to lead an army of eighty thousand men against Hannibal. It was the largest army the Romans had ever sent into battle. Hannibal completely surrounded the army and defeated it. Aemilius Paulus was killed in the battle.

Battle of Zama
Publius Cornelius Scipio and his army beat Hannibal. Hannibal managed to escape but most of his army was killed.